DESSERTS
with
Character

FRANCES BLAZEK & JOYCE CARTER

DESSERTS with *Character*

Published by Blazenspires, LLC

P.O. Box 2341

Frisco, Texas 75034

www.blazenspires.com

Designed by Frank Stanley Gove

ISBN 0-9722028-1-1

First Edition

Disclaimer: The Authors and Publisher expressly disclaim responsibility for any adverse effects arising directly or indirectly from information contained in this book.

Printed in the United States of America by Taylor Publishing Company, Dallas, Texas

Dedication

TO OUR PARENTS, WHO ARE TWO TRULY INSPIRATIONAL PEOPLE.

WE LOVE YOU BOTH DEARLY.

Acknowledgments

Just as a dessert recipe requires more than one ingredient, our book required the enthusiasm and commitment of a team of people. Part of our joy in producing this book was sharing the experience with so many wonderful people. They were the key ingredients in the process, and we extend our hearty thanks to them.

We are profoundly grateful to our family members who contributed their dessert recipes—they provided the foundation for this book. Our mother deserves special recognition for sharing her many delicious recipes and her years of baking expertise with us. As always, we appreciate her constant willingness to help.

Our book-cover designer and layout artist, Frank Stanley Gove, is a blessing. Not only did he design a beautiful book—inside and out—he also shared with us his comforting presence of mind. And thanks to our editors, Ann Farkas and Mindy Reed, for polishing our words and giving our book the important final touches.

Finally, from the bottom of our hearts, we express our appreciation to our immediate family. Their constant love and support are treasures that cannot be replaced. Without the encouragement of our oldest brother, Martin, and his wife, Karen, the book would not have evolved to this point. Blake, Joyce's dear husband, deserves a gold medal for his patience and understanding during our "marathon" weekends. Thanks to him for being such an understanding husband. We appreciate the creativity provided by our sister, Janet. Her ideas added spice to the book. And a special thanks to Ashlyn—our sweet little angel.

Contents

Foreword

The genesis of DESSERTS with *Character* was bittersweet. Through the years at various gatherings, Frances heard a recurring theme from others: "I wish I had Grandmother's recipe for...." Sadly, when these beloved women passed away, so did the tradition of having their special dishes at family get-togethers. No one ever took the time to capture on paper the recipes their grandmothers knew by heart.

Determined to preserve our family's tradition, Frances started collecting recipes and enlisted our mother's help. Gradually, Frances and Mom sifted through numerous "seasoned" recipes that Mom had accumulated over the years. These recipes were seasoned not only with a splash of vanilla and a pinch of cinnamon, but also with wise tips that Mom shared with Frances. With the help of Mom and our family, Frances created a timeless family cookbook that could be passed on from generation to generation.

Originally intended only for use by our immediate family, the keepsake has grown over time and is now shared by our extended family and friends. After several requests from people in the community, the special project has evolved even further.

Today, we have chosen some of our family's favorite recipes and compiled a new cookbook that we would like to share with you. Although we are neither baking gurus like our mother nor professional photographers, we wanted to create a family-inspired dessert book to pass on from generation to generation and from friend to friend. That is how DESSERTS with *Character* was born.

We hope this book creates many fond memories for you and your loved ones.

Warm regards,
Frances & Joyce

CANDIES & COOKIES

BONBONS

1 (14-ounce) package coconut, shredded
1 (14-ounce) can sweetened condensed milk
1/2 cup (1 stick) butter, softened
1 teaspoon vanilla
2 cups pecans, finely chopped
2 boxes (16 ounces each) confectioners' sugar
2 packages (24 ounces each) chocolate-flavored bark coating

- In a large mixing bowl, stir by hand the coconut, sweetened condensed milk, butter, vanilla, and pecans.

- Gradually add the confectioners' sugar. Stir the mixture until well blended.

- Shape into balls, and place onto an ungreased baking sheet.

- Place the baking sheet into the freezer until the balls are firm (about an hour).

- In a large nonstick saucepan on the stovetop, melt one package of the chocolate bark over low heat. Stir constantly until smooth. Remove from heat.
  Note: Repeat this step with the other package of chocolate bark when the coating runs out.

- Immediately dip the balls into the melted chocolate, fully covering each ball. Place onto wax paper.

  Tip: Use a toothpick to remove the balls from the chocolate. Then cover the toothpick hole with chocolate.

- Let the Bonbons harden for several hours before storing.

- Store in an airtight container, placing wax paper between the layers.

Yields approximately 100 Bonbons

10

Beauty

ALTHOUGH THE BONBON'S BEAUTIFUL EXTERIOR INITIALLY ATTRACTS US, IT IS THE INNER FILLING THAT LEAVES A GOOD TASTE IN OUR MOUTHS. 美麗

CHOCOLATE CARAMEL TURTLES

2 cups pecans, whole
2 tablespoons milk
1 (14-ounce) package caramels, unwrapped
6 squares (12 ounces) chocolate-flavored bark coating

- On two nonstick baking sheets, make the "feet" part of each turtle by placing four pecans into an "X" shape.
- In a large nonstick saucepan on the stovetop, combine the milk and caramels.
- Cook over low heat, stirring constantly, until the caramels are melted. Remove from heat.
- Drop the melted caramel mixture over each pecan cluster.
- Place the baking sheets into the freezer until the caramels harden.
- In a large nonstick saucepan on the stovetop, melt the chocolate bark over low heat. Stir constantly until smooth. Remove from heat.
- Immediately dip both sides of the firm caramel-coated pecans into the melted chocolate. Place onto wax paper.
- Let the Chocolate Caramel Turtles harden.
- Store in an airtight container, placing wax paper between the layers.

Yields approximately 24 Turtles

Patience

"MS. CHOCOLATE TURTLE" KNOWS THAT SHE WILL REACH
THE FINISH LINE ALL IN GOOD TIME. SHE HAS MASTERED THE
VIRTUE OF PATIENCE. 忍

CONGO SQUARES

3/4 cup (1 1/2 sticks) butter, softened
2 1/4 cups brown sugar, packed
3 eggs
2 3/4 cups flour
2 1/2 teaspoons baking powder
1/2 teaspoon salt
1 cup nuts, chopped
1 (12-ounce) package semisweet chocolate chips

14

• Preheat the oven to 350 degrees.

• In a large mixing bowl, beat the butter, brown sugar, and eggs.

• Gradually add the flour.

• Add the baking powder and salt. Blend well.

• Fold in the nuts and chocolate chips.

• Pour the batter into a greased 13 x 9 x 2-inch baking pan.

• Bake at 350 degrees for 30 to 35 minutes or until done.

• Let cool. Cut into squares.

Yields 20 to 24 Squares

Celebration

CELEBRATE! MIX SOME MUSIC, AND POUR YOUR HEART
INTO DANCING. 慶祝

DATE BALLS

3 cups crispy rice cereal
1/2 cup nuts, chopped
1/4 cup (1/2 stick) butter
3/4 cup sugar
2 eggs, slightly beaten
1 1/2 cups pitted dates, chopped
1 cup coconut

- In a large mixing bowl, mix the crispy rice cereal and nuts together. Set aside.
- In a large nonstick saucepan on the stovetop, melt the butter over medium heat
- Add the sugar, beaten eggs, and dates, stirring constantly for 8 to 10 minutes.
- Mash the dates as they cook. Remove from heat.
- Pour the hot mixture over the crispy rice cereal. Mix well.
- Shape into balls, and roll in the coconut.
- Place the Date Balls onto wax paper to cool.

Yields 24 to 30 Balls

Romance

DATES MAY

SNOWBALL INTO

TRUE ROMANCE

BY BEING YOURSELF —

NOT SOMEONE

ELSE.

浪漫

Spirit

MAY YOUR DIVINE SPIRIT ALWAYS BE WITHIN YOU.

精神

DIVINITY

2 cups sugar
1/2 cup water
1/8 teaspoon salt
1 (7-ounce) jar marshmallow crème
3/4 cup nuts, chopped
1 teaspoon vanilla

- In a large saucepan on the stovetop, dissolve the sugar, water, and salt over medium heat.
- Bring to a boil for 2 minutes, stirring constantly.
- Place the marshmallow crème into a large mixing bowl.
- Pour the hot mixture over the marshmallow crème. Carefully stir with a spoon.
- Using a mixer, beat the mixture on high speed for about 4 minutes.
- Fold in the nuts. Add the vanilla.
- Drop by spoonfuls onto wax paper.
- Let the Divinity set for several hours to harden.
- Store in an airtight container, placing wax paper between the layers.

Yields approximately 24 candies

DOUBLE CHOCOLATE BROWNIES

BROWNIES

2 cups sugar
2 cups flour
1 teaspoon baking soda
1 cup (2 sticks) butter
4 tablespoons cocoa
1 cup water
1/2 cup buttermilk
2 eggs
1 teaspoon vanilla

FROSTING

1/2 cup (1 stick) butter
4 tablespoons cocoa
6 tablespoons buttermilk
1 (16-ounce) box confectioners' sugar
1 teaspoon vanilla
1 cup nuts

BROWNIES

- Preheat the oven to 350 degrees.
- In a large mixing bowl, combine the sugar, flour, and baking soda. Set aside.
- In a large saucepan on the stovetop, combine the butter, cocoa, and water. Cook over medium heat, and stir well.
- Bring to a boil, stirring constantly. Remove from heat.
- Gradually pour the cocoa mixture into the flour mixture. Stir until smooth.
- Add the buttermilk, eggs, and vanilla. Beat well.
- Pour the batter into a greased jelly-roll pan (15 x 10 inches) or onto a baking sheet with 1/2-inch sides.
- Bake at 350 degrees for 20 minutes or until done.
- Leave in the pan. Spread the frosting while both the Brownies and frosting are still warm.

FROSTING

- In a medium saucepan on the stovetop, melt the butter. Add the cocoa and buttermilk.
- Bring to a rapid boil, stirring constantly. Remove from heat.
- Add the confectioners' sugar, vanilla, and nuts. Stir until smooth.

Yields approximately 24 Brownies

Successful

SUCCESS STARTS WITH A SOLID FOUNDATION AND

BUILDS ONE STEP AT A TIME.

Confidence

CONFIDENCE DOES NOT HAVE THE RIGHT ANSWERS—
JUST THE RIGHT ATTITUDE. 自信

HONEY CRISPY TREATS

1/2 **cup honey**

1/2 **cup sugar**

1 cup peanut butter, creamy or crunchy

2 cups crispy rice cereal

- In a large saucepan on the stovetop, combine the honey and sugar.

- Cook over medium heat, stirring constantly.

- Bring to a boil (about 1 minute). Remove from heat.

- Add the peanut butter and crispy rice cereal. Stir until well blended.

- Drop by spoonfuls onto an ungreased baking sheet.

- Place the baking sheet into the freezer until the Treats set. Remove when firm (about 10 minutes).

Yields approximately 24 Treats

LEMON COCONUT COOKIES

1/4 cup (1/2 stick) butter, softened
1/4 cup shortening
1 cup sugar
1 egg
2 tablespoons lemon rind, grated
3/4 cup coconut, shredded
1 3/4 cups flour
1/2 teaspoon salt
2 tablespoons baking powder

- In a large mixing bowl, beat the butter, shortening, sugar, and egg.
- Add the grated lemon and coconut.
- Combine the flour, salt, and baking powder in a separate bowl.
- Gradually add the flour mixture to the creamed lemon mixture. Blend well.
- With floured hands, shape the dough into two long rolls, and place onto wax paper.
- Place the cookie dough into the freezer for a couple of hours.
- Once the cookie dough becomes firm, preheat the oven to 375 degrees.
- Remove the dough from the freezer, and thinly slice the rolls with a knife.
- Place the slices onto a greased baking sheet.
- Bake at 375 degrees for 10 to 12 minutes or until light brown.

Yields approximately 4 dozen

Serenity

WHEN FEELING

OVERWHELMED,

FIND A PEACEFUL

PLACE TO UNWIND.

平靜

MARSHMALLOW ALMOND BALLS

3 cups almonds, finely chopped

3 cups coconut, shredded

1 (7-ounce) jar marshmallow crème

1 (14-ounce) can sweetened condensed milk

1 (12-ounce) package semisweet chocolate chips

1 (16-ounce) bag large marshmallows

26

- In a medium bowl, combine the almonds and coconut. Set aside.

- In a large nonstick saucepan on the stovetop, combine the marshmallow crème, sweetened condensed milk, and chocolate chips.

- Melt over low heat, stirring often. Remove from heat.

- Dip each marshmallow into the chocolate mixture, and roll in the almond/coconut mixture.

- Place the Marshmallow Almond Balls onto wax paper to set.

Yields 65 to 70 Balls

Persistence

PERSISTENCE IS THE ENDLESS ABILITY TO BOUNCE BACK
FROM REJECTION, TIME AND TIME AGAIN.

OVEN-CARAMEL POPCORN

3 quarts popcorn, popped
1 cup brown sugar, packed
1/2 cup (1 stick) butter
1/2 cup light corn syrup
1/2 teaspoon vanilla
1/2 teaspoon baking soda
1 cup roasted peanuts

28

- Preheat the oven to 250 degrees.
- Place the popcorn in a large shallow roasting pan coated with cooking spray.
- In a large saucepan on the stovetop, combine the brown sugar, butter, and corn syrup.
- Bring to a boil over medium heat, stirring constantly.
- Then, without stirring, let the sugar coating boil for 5 minutes. Remove from heat.
- Add the vanilla, baking soda, and peanuts. Mix well.
- Pour the sugar coating over the popcorn. Stir the popcorn well.
- Bake at 250 degrees for 60 minutes, stirring the popcorn every 15 minutes.
- Spoon the Oven-Caramel Popcorn onto a large piece of foil. Break the Popcorn apart as it cools.

Yields approximately 3 quarts

Friends

SOME OF YOUR FRIENDS MAY COME AND GO, BUT THEY ARE
PUT IN YOUR LIFE AT CERTAIN TIMES FOR A REASON. 朋友

Fate

YOU WILL KNOW FATE IS REAL WHEN YOU REALIZE THE
EVENTS IN YOUR LIFE WERE NOT RANDOM—THEY ARE
ALL CONNECTED TO A HIGHER CAUSE.　命

PEANUT BUTTER BARS

BARS
3/4 **stick butter, softened**
1/3 **cup light brown sugar**
1/4 **cup sugar**
1 egg
1/3 **cup creamy peanut butter**
1/2 **teaspoon baking soda**
1/2 **teaspoon vanilla**
1 cup flour
1/8 **teaspoon salt**
1 cup and 3 tablespoons raw quick-cooking oats

GLAZE
1/4 **cup creamy peanut butter**
2 cups confectioners' sugar
1/3 **cup milk**

BARS
- Preheat the oven to 325 degrees.

- In a large mixing bowl, beat the butter, brown sugar, sugar, egg, and peanut butter.

- Add the baking soda, vanilla, flour, and salt. Blend well.

- Fold in the raw oats.

- Press the dough onto a greased 13 x 9 x 2-inch baking pan until the bottom of the pan is covered evenly.

- Bake at 325 degrees for 18 to 20 minutes or until brown around the edges.

- Let cool. Spread the glaze on top of the Bars and cut into squares.

GLAZE
- In a medium bowl, combine the peanut butter, confectioners' sugar, and milk until smooth.

Tip: If the glaze is too thick, then add more milk. If it is too thin, then add more confectioners' sugar.

Yields 16 to 20 Bars

PEANUT WALNUT CLUSTERS

1 cup semisweet or milk chocolate chips

1/2 cup peanut butter, creamy or crunchy

1 cup roasted peanuts

1/2 cup walnuts, chopped

- In a large bowl, melt the chocolate chips in the microwave for 1 to 2 minutes, stirring halfway through. *Note: Use a microwave-safe bowl. Tip: The chocolate chips may also be melted in a nonstick saucepan on the stovetop.*

- Add the peanut butter, peanuts, and walnuts. Stir until well blended.

- Drop by spoonfuls onto a baking sheet covered with wax paper.

- Place the baking sheet into the freezer until the Clusters set. Remove when firm (about 10 minutes).

Yields approximately 30 Clusters

Family

EVEN THOUGH A PEANUT CAN EXIST BY ITSELF, IT'S THE PEANUTS
THAT CLUSTER TOGETHER THAT STAY TOGETHER.

PECAN PUFFS

1 egg white

1 cup light brown sugar, packed

1/4 teaspoon salt

1/4 teaspoon baking soda

2 1/2 cups pecans, finely chopped

- Preheat the oven to 300 degrees.

- In a large mixing bowl, beat the egg white on high speed until stiff or until peaks start to form.

- Add the brown sugar, salt, and baking soda. Blend well.

- Fold in the pecans.

- Drop by spoonfuls onto a baking sheet coated with cooking spray.

- Bake at 300 degrees for 20 minutes or until done.

Yields approximately 24 Puffs

Health

A SIMPLE STROLL THROUGH THE PARK DOES WONDERS

FOR OUR MENTAL AND PHYSICAL HEALTH.

Courage

A LITTLE COURAGE CAN UNCOVER EXCITING

NEW FRONTIERS. 勇氣

RANGER COOKIES

1 cup (2 sticks) butter, softened
1 cup light brown sugar, packed
1 cup sugar
2 eggs
2 cups corn flakes
2 cups raw quick-cooking oats
2 cups flour
1 teaspoon baking soda
1 teaspoon baking powder
1 teaspoon vanilla

OPTIONAL
1 cup raisins
1 (12-ounce) package semisweet chocolate, milk chocolate,
or butterscotch chips

- Preheat the oven to 350 degrees.

- In a large mixing bowl, beat the butter, brown sugar, sugar, and eggs.

- Add the corn flakes, raw oats, flour, baking soda, baking powder, and vanilla.
  Blend well.

- Add the optional ingredients of your choice.

- Drop by spoonfuls onto a greased baking sheet.

- Bake at 350 degrees for 8 to 10 minutes or until light brown.

Yields approximately 5 dozen

RUM BALLS

1 cup vanilla wafers, crushed

1 1/3 cups confectioners' sugar

1 1/2 cups nuts, chopped

2 tablespoons cocoa

2 tablespoons light corn syrup

1/4 cup liquor—vanilla rum

38

- In a large mixing bowl, combine the crushed vanilla wafers, 1 cup confectioners' sugar, and nuts.

- Add the cocoa, corn syrup, and liquor. Mix well.

- Form small balls—the smaller the better. Place onto wax paper.

- Roll the formed balls in the remaining (1/3 cup) confectioners' sugar.

- Place the Rum Balls into an airtight container. Store in a cool place.

Note: Since the Rum Balls contain alcohol, consume responsibly.

Variation: Rum-flavored extract may be substituted for the rum liquor.

Yields approximately 35 Balls

Balance

LIFE IS A CONSTANT BALANCING ACT. TOO MUCH OF ONE
THING CAN LEAD TO CHAOS.　　均衡

SEVEN-MINUTE FUDGE

1 cup (2 sticks) butter
4 1/2 cups sugar
1 (5-ounce) can evaporated milk
3 (1 ounce each) semisweet baking chocolate squares
1 (10 1/2-ounce) package miniature marshmallows
1 (12-ounce) package semisweet chocolate chips
1 teaspoon vanilla
1 cup pecans, chopped

- In a large 6-quart saucepan on the stovetop, combine the butter, sugar, and evaporated milk.

- Cooking over medium heat, bring to a boil. Stir constantly.

- Allow to boil for 7 minutes, still stirring constantly.

- Remove from heat.

- Add the chocolate squares, marshmallows, and chocolate chips. Stir until dissolved.

- Add the vanilla and pecans.

- Pour the fudge mixture into an ungreased jelly-roll pan (15 x 10 inches).

- Allow the Fudge to harden for several hours, and cut into squares.

Yields approximately 35 squares

Honesty

ALTHOUGH SOMETIMES WE ARE TEMPTED TO FUDGE
THE TRUTH, SIMPLE HONESTY AVOIDS FUTURE
STICKY SITUATIONS. 誠實

SHOESTRING POTATO CANDIES

1 (11-ounce) package butterscotch chips
3 tablespoons crunchy peanut butter
2 cups shoestring potato chips
1/2 cup nuts, chopped

• In a large nonstick saucepan on the stovetop, melt the butterscotch chips and peanut butter over low heat until smooth. Stir constantly.

• Remove from heat. Add the shoestring potato chips and nuts. Stir well.

• Drop by spoonfuls onto a baking sheet covered with wax paper.

• Place the baking sheet into the freezer until the Candies set. Remove when firm (about 10 minutes).

Yields 16 to 20 Candies

Creativity

A SHOESTRING BUDGET UNTIES CREATIVITY.

創造力

SNICKERDOODLES

1/2 cup (1 stick) butter, softened
1 cup sugar
1 egg
1 1/3 cups flour
1 teaspoon cream of tartar
1/2 teaspoon baking soda
1/4 teaspoon salt
1/2 teaspoon cinnamon

- Preheat the oven to 375 degrees.

- In a large mixing bowl, beat the butter, 3/4 cup sugar, and egg.

- Add the flour, cream of tartar, baking soda, and salt. Blend well.

- Form the cookie dough into small balls.
  Note: The cookie dough should be soft.

- Combine the cinnamon and remaining sugar (1/4 cup) in a small bowl.

- Roll the balls in the sugar/cinnamon mixture to coat.

- Place the coated balls onto a greased baking sheet, and flatten slightly.

- Bake at 375 degrees for 8 to 10 minutes or until the edges are slightly browned.

Yields 2 to 2 1/2 dozen

Laugh

SMILE! GIGGLE! PLAY! UNLEASH THE CHILD WITHIN.

SPICY SUGARED NUTS

1 cup sugar
1/2 cup water
1 teaspoon salt
2 teaspoons cinnamon
1/2 teaspoon cloves
2 cups nuts, whole

46

- In a large saucepan on the stovetop, combine the candy coating—sugar, water, salt, cinnamon, and cloves.

- Cook over medium heat, stirring constantly until the candy coating reaches soft-ball stage. *(See "Hints.")*

- Remove from heat. Add the nuts.

- Stir until the nuts are well coated.

- Quickly turn the nuts onto waxed paper.

- Separate the Spicy Sugared Nuts. Let cool.

Yields approximately 2 cups

 Energy

SPICE UP YOUR LIFE BY FOCUSING YOUR ENERGY ON THE

THINGS THAT REALLY MATTER.

Affection

SIMPLE, SWEET KISSES ARE INEXPENSIVE SIGNS OF AFFECTION.

SWEET KISSES

4 egg whites
3/4 cup sugar
1/8 teaspoon salt
1/4 teaspoon cream of tartar
1/2 teaspoon vanilla
1/2 cup coconut, shredded
1/2 cup nuts, chopped
3 cups corn flakes

• Preheat the oven to 300 degrees.

• In a large mixing bowl, beat the egg whites on high speed until stiff or until peaks start to form.

• Add the sugar, salt, cream of tartar, and vanilla. Blend well.

• Fold in the coconut, nuts, and corn flakes.

• Drop by spoonfuls onto a greased baking sheet.

• Bake at 300 degrees for 18 to 20 minutes or until lightly browned.

Yields approximately 30 Kisses

UNBAKED OATMEAL COOKIES

4 tablespoons cocoa
2 cups sugar
1/2 cup (1 stick) butter
1/2 cup milk
1 teaspoon vanilla
1/2 cup crunchy peanut butter
2 cups raw quick-cooking oats
1 cup coconut, shredded
1 cup nuts, chopped (optional)

• In a large saucepan on the stovetop, combine the cocoa, sugar, butter, and milk.

• Cook over medium heat, stirring constantly, until boiling.

• Boil for 1 1/2 minutes.

• Remove from heat.

• Add the vanilla, peanut butter, raw oats, and coconut. Add the nuts, if desired. Stir until well blended.

• Drop by spoonfuls onto an ungreased baking sheet.

• Place the baking sheet into the freezer until the Cookies set. Remove when firm (about 10 minutes).

Yields approximately 2 dozen

Unique

SOMETIMES UNCONVENTIONAL METHODS OFFER THE SUPERIOR SOLUTION.　獨特

WHITE BARK TREATS

2 pounds (32 ounces) white bark coating

1 cup crunchy peanut butter

2 cups miniature marshmallows

3 cups crispy rice cereal

2 cups dry roasted peanuts

- Preheat the oven to 200 degrees.
- Melt the white bark in a 13 x 9 x 2-inch baking pan in the oven (about 15 to 20 minutes). Stir every 5 minutes.
- Remove the melted white bark from the oven.
- Add the peanut butter, and stir until smooth.
- In a very large mixing bowl, combine the marshmallows, crispy rice cereal, and peanuts.
- Pour the hot bark mixture over the crispy rice mixture. Stir well.
- Drop by spoonfuls onto wax paper.
- Let the White Bark Treats harden.
- Store in an airtight container, placing wax paper between the layers.

Yields approximately 72 Treats

Respect

WHEN GOING THROUGH CHALLENGING TIMES, REFRAIN
FROM BARKING AT OTHERS. YOU OPEN THE GATE OF
RESPECT BY TAKING A DEEP BREATH AND
REMAINING CALM. 尊敬

PIES

Opportunity

WE LOVE THE APPLE-AMERICAN PIE BECAUSE IT REPRESENTS A SLICE OF OPPORTUNITY. 機會

APPLE-AMERICAN PIE

3 to 4 apples, cored and sliced
1 cup sugar
1/2 cup flour
1 to 2 teaspoons cinnamon
2 tablespoons butter, softened
2 (9-inch) deep-dish piecrusts, unbaked

- Preheat the oven to 375 degrees.

- In a large mixing bowl, gently stir the apples, sugar, flour, cinnamon, and butter, until the apples are well coated.

- Pour the apple mixture into the bottom piecrust.

- Place the other piecrust on top of the pie, and flute the edges.

- Cut several slits in the top piecrust.

- Bake at 375 degrees for 30 to 35 minutes or until the crust is golden brown.

- Serve with your favorite vanilla ice cream, if desired.

Serves 8

BLACKBERRY DELIGHT PIE

2 cups blackberries (fresh or frozen)
1/2 cup sugar
1/2 cup flour
2 (9-inch) piecrusts, unbaked
1 tablespoon butter

• Preheat the oven to 375 degrees.

• In a large mixing bowl, gently stir the blackberries, sugar, and flour, until the blackberries are well coated.

• Pour the blackberry mixture into the bottom piecrust.

• Dot with butter. Place the other piecrust on top of the pie, and flute the edges.

• Cut several slits in the top piecrust.

• Bake at 375 degrees for 30 to 35 minutes or until the crust is golden brown.

• Serve with your favorite vanilla ice cream, if desired.

Tip: If using frozen blackberries, be sure to thaw and drain them before preparing the pie.

Serves 8

Protection

SOMETIMES THE PRICKLY THORN IN OUR SIDE IS THERE FOR OUR OWN PROTECTION.

保護

MILLION DOLLAR PIE

1 (8-ounce) can crushed pineapple, drained
1 (14-ounce) can sweetened condensed milk
1/3 cup lemon juice
1 cup nuts, chopped
1 cup coconut, shredded
1 (8-ounce) container frozen whipped topping, slightly thawed
1 (9-inch) piecrust, baked

- In a large mixing bowl, combine the pineapple, sweetened condensed milk, and lemon juice.

- Fold in the nuts, coconut, and whipped topping. Stir well.

- Pour the whipped topping mixture into the baked piecrust.

- Cover and refrigerate for at least 1 hour before serving.

- Refrigerate the leftovers.

Serves 8

Wealth

WEALTH IS MEASURED BY THE NUMBER OF LIVES YOU TOUCH.

PEACH PIE

2 cups peaches, sliced (fresh or frozen)

1/2 cup sugar

1/2 cup flour

2 (9-inch) piecrusts, unbaked

1/8 teaspoon cinnamon

1 tablespoon butter

- Preheat the oven to 375 degrees.
- In a large mixing bowl, gently stir the peaches, sugar, and flour, until the peaches are well coated.
- Pour the peach mixture into the bottom piecrust.
- Sprinkle with cinnamon and dot with butter.
- Place the other piecrust on top of the pie, and flute the edges.
- Cut several slits in the top piecrust.
- Bake at 375 degrees for 30 to 35 minutes or until the crust is golden brown.
- Serve with your favorite vanilla ice cream, if desired.

Tip: If using frozen peaches, be sure to thaw and drain the peaches before preparing the pie.

Serves 8

Optimistic

PEACH FOR THE STARS—IF YOU FALL SHORT, YOU ARE
STILL FARTHER AHEAD. 樂觀

PECAN-CHOCOLATE PIE

3 eggs
1 cup dark corn syrup
1/2 cup sugar
1/4 cup (1/2 stick) butter, melted
1 teaspoon vanilla
1/4 teaspoon salt
1 tablespoon flour
1 cup pecans, chopped
1/2 cup semisweet chocolate chips
1 (9-inch) deep-dish piecrust, unbaked

- Preheat the oven to 350 degrees.

- In a large mixing bowl, beat the eggs, corn syrup, sugar, butter, vanilla, salt, and flour until well blended.

- Fold in the pecans and chocolate chips.

- Pour the pecan-chocolate mixture into the piecrust.

- Bake at 350 degrees for 50 to 55 minutes or until firm.

Serves 8

Loyal

WE ALL KNOW THAT CERTAIN RECIPES ARE ALWAYS

LOYAL—THEY NEVER FAIL US, ESPECIALLY WHEN

WE NEED THEM MOST.　忠誠

PINEAPPLE COCONUT PIE

1 1/2 **cups sugar**
3 **tablespoons flour**
3 **eggs**
1/2 **cup (1 stick) butter, melted**
1 **teaspoon lemon juice**
1 **teaspoon vanilla**
1 **(8-ounce) can crushed pineapple, undrained**
1 **cup coconut, shredded**
1 **(9-inch) deep-dish piecrust, unbaked**

66

- Preheat the oven to 350 degrees.

- In a large mixing bowl, beat the sugar, flour, eggs, and butter. Blend well.

- Add the lemon juice and vanilla.

- Fold in the pineapple and coconut.

- Pour the pineapple mixture into the piecrust.

- Bake at 350 degrees for 45 to 50 minutes or until firm and golden brown.

Serves 8

Paradise

THE SOUND OF THE OCEAN KISSING THE SOFT, SANDY BEACH

TRANSFORMS A NOISY DAY INTO PARADISE.
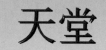

Wisdom

THE OLD AND SHRIVELED FRUIT HOLDS MORE SUNSHINE
AND WISDOM THAN THE BUDDING YOUNG GRAPE.

RAISIN-PECAN PIE

2 eggs
1 cup sugar
1 tablespoon flour
1/4 cup (1/2 stick) butter, softened
1 teaspoon allspice
1/2 cup raisins
1/2 cup pecans, chopped
1 (9-inch) piecrust, unbaked

- Preheat the oven to 350 degrees.

- In a large mixing bowl, beat the eggs, sugar, flour, butter, and allspice until well blended.

- Fold in the raisins and pecans.

- Pour the raisin-pecan mixture into the piecrust.

- Bake at 350 degrees for 30 minutes or until firm.

Serves 8

SILKY CHOCOLATE PIE

2 cups milk
1/2 cup flour
1 cup sugar
1/3 cup cocoa
3 egg yolks, slightly beaten
1 tablespoon butter
1 teaspoon vanilla
1 (9-inch) piecrust, baked

70

- In a large saucepan on the stovetop, cook the milk, flour, sugar, cocoa, and egg yolks over medium heat until thick.

- Remove from heat.

- Add the butter and vanilla. Stir well.

- Spoon the chocolate filling into the baked piecrust.

- Cool the pie completely, then refrigerate.

Serves 8

Intuition

A WOMAN'S INTUITION IS NEVER WRONG. TRUST IT!

直覺

TROPICAL CREAM PIE

3/4 **cup sugar**

3 tablespoons cornstarch

2 cups milk

3 egg yolks, slightly beaten

2 tablespoons butter

1 teaspoon vanilla

1 (9-inch) piecrust, baked

- In a large saucepan on the stovetop, combine the sugar, cornstarch, and milk.
- Cook over medium heat, and bring to a boil, stirring constantly.
- In a small bowl, mix about 1/3 cup of the hot mixture with the egg yolks, beating slightly, to avoid curdling.
- Pour the egg mixture into the rest of the hot mixture in the saucepan. Blend well.
- Bring to a boil for 2 minutes.
- Remove from heat, and add the butter and vanilla.
- Add the variations, if desired. Stir well.
- Pour the mixture into the baked piecrust.
- Cool the pie completely, then refrigerate.

VARIATIONS
- Add 1 sliced banana or 1 (8-ounce) can crushed pineapple, drained.
- Add 1/2 cup nuts or 1/2 cup coconut.

Serves 8

Change

EMBRACE CHANGE—IT ENRICHES YOUR LIFE.

CAKES

ANGEL'S HEAVENLY FOOD

1 box angel food cake mix

1 (12-ounce) container frozen whipped topping, slightly thawed

2 cups fresh strawberries, stemmed and sliced

1 cup fresh blueberries, whole

- Using the ingredients listed on the cake box, prepare the cake. Bake as directed.

- Cool the cake completely.

- In a trifle bowl, tear pieces of the angel food cake, and layer them on the bottom of the bowl.

- Layer half of the whipped topping over the angel food pieces.

- Layer half of the strawberries over the whipped topping.

- Sprinkle half of the blueberries over the strawberries.

- Repeat the layers of angel food pieces, whipped topping, strawberries, and blueberries.

- Cover and refrigerate.

Serves approximately 12

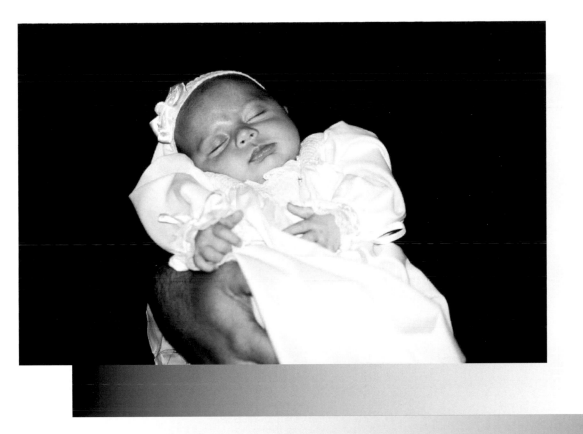

Angel

YOUR ANGEL IS ALWAYS THERE TO GUARD YOU ALONG

YOUR DARKEST PATHS.   天使

APPLESAUCE WALNUT CAKE

1 1/2 cups sugar
1/2 cup (1 stick) butter, softened
2 eggs
2 cups applesauce
2 cups flour
1 teaspoon baking soda
1 teaspoon cinnamon
1 teaspoon allspice
1/8 teaspoon salt
1 cup raisins
1 cup walnuts, chopped

• Preheat the oven to 375 degrees.

• In a large mixing bowl, beat the sugar, butter, and eggs.

• Add the applesauce, flour, baking soda, cinnamon, allspice, and salt. Blend well.

• Fold in the raisins and walnuts.

• Pour the batter into a prepared Bundt pan.

• Bake at 375 degrees for 55 to 60 minutes or until done.

• Cool the cake in the pan on a wire rack for 10 minutes. Remove from the pan.

Serves 10 to 12

Circle

LIFE IS A FULL CIRCLE. AS BABIES, OTHERS FEED US APPLESAUCE. AS WE MATURE, WE FEED OURSELVES APPLES. AS WE COME FULL CIRCLE, OTHERS FEED US APPLESAUCE AGAIN.

循環

BANANA NUT CAKE

CAKE

2 eggs
1/2 cup (1 stick) butter, softened
1 1/2 cups sugar
2/3 cup buttermilk
1 cup bananas, mashed
1 teaspoon lemon juice
2 1/4 cups flour
2 teaspoons baking powder
1/2 teaspoon baking soda
1 teaspoon salt
1 teaspoon vanilla
3/4 cup nuts, chopped

FROSTING

1 tablespoon butter
1 banana, mashed
1 (16-ounce) box confectioners' sugar

CAKE

- Preheat the oven to 350 degrees.
- In a large mixing bowl, beat the eggs, butter, sugar, buttermilk, bananas, and lemon juice.
- Add the flour, baking powder, baking soda, salt, and vanilla. Blend well.
- Fold in 1/2 cup of nuts.
- Pour the batter into a prepared 13 x 9 x 2-inch baking pan.
- Bake at 350 degrees for 30 to 35 minutes or until done.
- Cool the cake in the pan on a wire rack for 10 minutes. Remove from the pan.
- Cool the cake completely, then smooth with the frosting.
- Sprinkle the remaining nuts (1/4 cup) on top of the cake.

FROSTING

- In a medium bowl, combine the butter, banana, and confectioners' sugar until well blended.

Serves 12 to 24

Passion

FIND YOUR PASSION IN LIFE, AND GO BANANAS!

BIRTHDAY CAKE

2 eggs
1 1/3 cups sugar
1/2 cup (1 stick) butter, softened
1 cup milk
2 cups flour
2 1/2 teaspoons baking powder
3/4 teaspoon salt
1 teaspoon vanilla
frosting of your choice

- Preheat the oven to 350 degrees.
- In a large mixing bowl, beat the eggs, sugar, butter, and milk.
- Add the flour, baking powder, salt, and vanilla. Blend well.
- Pour equal amounts of the batter into two prepared 9-inch round pans.
- Bake at 350 degrees for 25 to 30 minutes or until done.
- Cool each cake in its pan on a wire rack for 10 minutes.
- Remove from the pans, and cool completely.
- Before layering the cakes, frost the top of the bottom cake with the frosting.
- Layer the second cake on top of the bottom cake. Then frost the entire Birthday Cake.
- Serve with your favorite ice cream.

Serves 12

Life

BIRTHDAYS REMIND US TO CELEBRATE THE

MIRACLE OF LIFE.

CARROT CAKE

CAKE

1 cup sugar
1 cup oil
3 eggs
1 teaspoon salt
1 1/3 cups flour
1 1/3 teaspoons baking soda
1 1/3 teaspoons baking powder
1 1/3 teaspoons cinnamon
2 cups carrots, grated
3/4 cup raisins
1/2 cup nuts, chopped (optional)

FROSTING

1 (8-ounce) package cream cheese, softened
1/2 cup (1 stick) butter, softened
1 (16-ounce) box confectioners' sugar
1 teaspoon vanilla

CAKE

- Preheat the oven to 325 degrees.
- In a large mixing bowl, beat the sugar, oil, and eggs.
- Add the dry ingredients—salt, flour, baking soda, baking powder, and cinnamon. Blend well.
- Fold in the carrots and raisins. Add the nuts, if desired.
- Pour the batter into a prepared 13 x 9 x 2-inch baking pan.
- Bake at 325 degrees for 50 to 55 minutes or until done.
- Cool the cake in the pan on a wire rack for 10 minutes. Remove from the pan.
- Cool the cake completely, then smooth with the frosting.
- Let the frosted cake set, then refrigerate.

FROSTING

- In a medium mixing bowl, beat the cream cheese, butter, confectioners' sugar, and vanilla. Mix well.

Serves 12 to 24

Dreamer

THE VISION OF TOMORROW IS HELD

IN THE EYES OF THE DREAMER. 夢想家

Good Work

RECOGNIZE AND REWARD OTHERS FOR THEIR GOOD WORK.

做的好

CHOCOLATE CHIP COOKIE CHEESECAKE

2 rolls (18 ounces each) chocolate chip cookie dough
1 cup sugar
1 egg
1 tablespoon vanilla
2 packages (8 ounces each) cream cheese, softened

- Preheat the oven to 350 degrees.

- Slice one cookie dough roll into small pieces, and layer the dough on the bottom of an ungreased 13 x 9 x 2-inch baking pan.

- In a large mixing bowl, beat the sugar, egg, vanilla, and cream cheese. Blend well.

- Spread the cream cheese mixture over the layered cookie dough.

- Slice the other cookie dough roll into small pieces, and layer the dough over the cream cheese mixture.

- Bake at 350 degrees for 35 to 40 minutes.
  Note: Do not overbake.

- Cool the Cheesecake completely, then refrigerate.

Serves 12 to 24

EARTHQUAKE CAKE

1 (7-ounce) package coconut, shredded
1 1/2 cups nuts, chopped
1 box German chocolate cake mix
1 (8-ounce) package cream cheese, softened
1/2 cup (1 stick) butter, softened
1 (16-ounce) box confectioners' sugar
1 teaspoon vanilla

- Preheat the oven to 350 degrees.

- Coat a 13 x 9 x 2-inch baking pan with cooking spray.

- Spread the coconut and nuts onto the bottom of the pan.

- Using the ingredients listed on the cake box, prepare the cake mix.
  Beat as directed.

- Pour the prepared cake mix evenly over the coconut and nuts.
  Important: Do not stir.

- In another large mixing bowl, beat the cream cheese, butter, confectioners'
  sugar, and vanilla until smooth.

- Spoon the mixture evenly on top of the cake mix. *Important: Do not stir.*

- Bake at 350 degrees for 45 to 55 minutes or until done.

- Cool the cake completely in the pan.

- Refrigerate the leftovers.

Serves 12 to 24

Crisis & Opportunity

ALTHOUGH A TRYING

EVENT MAY ROCK

YOUR LIFE, VIEW THE

EVENT AS AN

OPPORTUNITY, NOT

AS A SETBACK.

危機與轉機

ITALIAN CREAM CAKE

CAKE

2 cups sugar
1/2 cup oil
1/2 cup (1 stick) butter, softened
4 eggs, separated
1 cup buttermilk
1 teaspoon baking soda
2 cups flour
1 teaspoon vanilla
1 cup pecans, chopped
2 cups coconut, shredded

FROSTING

1 (8-ounce) package cream cheese, softened
1/2 cup (1 stick) butter, softened
1 (16-ounce) box confectioners' sugar
1 teaspoon vanilla

CAKE

- Preheat the oven to 350 degrees.
- In a large mixing bowl, beat the sugar, oil, butter, and egg yolks.
- Add the buttermilk, baking soda, flour, and vanilla. Blend well.
- In a separate bowl, beat the egg whites on high speed until stiff or until peaks start to form. Fold the stiffly beaten egg whites into the creamed mixture.
- Fold in the pecans and coconut.
- Pour the batter into a prepared 13 x 9 x 2-inch baking pan.
- Bake at 350 degrees for 35 to 40 minutes or until done.
- Cool the cake in the pan on a wire rack for 10 minutes. Remove from the pan.
- Cool the cake completely, then smooth with the frosting.
- Let the frosted cake set, then refrigerate.

FROSTING

- In a medium mixing bowl, beat the cream cheese, butter, confectioners' sugar, and vanilla until smooth.

Serves 12 to 24

Love

LOVE . . . SIMPLY SPREAD IT.

MUD CAKE

CAKE

1/2 cup (1 stick) butter, softened
1 cup sugar
1 teaspoon vanilla
3 eggs
3/4 cup flour
1/3 cup cocoa
1/2 teaspoon baking powder
1/8 teaspoon salt
1 cup nuts, chopped
1 (10 1/2-ounce) package miniature marshmallows

FROSTING

3/4 stick butter, softened
1/2 cup cocoa
2 2/3 cups confectioners' sugar
1/3 cup milk
1 teaspoon vanilla

CAKE

- Preheat the oven to 350 degrees.
- In a large mixing bowl, beat the butter, sugar, vanilla, and eggs.
- In a medium bowl, combine the dry ingredients—flour, cocoa, baking powder, and salt.
- Gradually add the dry ingredients to the creamed mixture. Blend well.
- Fold in the nuts.
- Pour the batter into a prepared 13 x 9 x 2-inch baking pan.
- Bake at 350 degrees for 25 to 30 minutes or until done.
- Remove the cake from the oven. Immediately spread the marshmallows over the cake.
- Place the cake back into the oven until the marshmallows start to melt (about 4 to 5 minutes).
- Remove the cake from the oven. Using a spoon, swirl the frosting into the marshmallows.
- Cool the cake completely in the pan, and cut into squares.

FROSTING

- In a medium mixing bowl, beat the butter, cocoa, confectioners' sugar, milk, and vanilla until smooth.

Serves 12 to 24

Forgiveness

ALTHOUGH SOMETIMES WE FALL VICTIM TO "MUDSLINGING,"

TAKE THE HIGH ROAD, AND FORGIVE THOSE WHO HAVE

HURT YOU. 寬恕

Flower

BLOOM! OPEN UP, AND BRIGHTEN SOMEONE ELSE'S DAY.

花

POPPY SEED CAKE

CAKE

6 eggs
2 cups sugar
1 1/2 cups flour
4 teaspoons baking powder
1 teaspoon salt
1 teaspoon vanilla
2 medium bananas, mashed
1 (12 1/2-ounce) can poppy seed filling
1 cup nuts, chopped (optional)
1 cup coconut, shredded (optional)

GLAZE

1 cup confectioners' sugar
2 tablespoons milk
1 teaspoon vanilla

CAKE

- Preheat the oven to 375 degrees.
- In a large mixing bowl, beat the eggs and sugar.
- Gradually add the flour.
- Add the baking powder, salt, and vanilla. Blend well.
- Fold in the bananas and poppy seed filling.
- Add the nuts and/or coconut, if desired.
- Pour the batter into a prepared 13 x 9 x 2-inch baking pan.
- Bake at 375 degrees for 30 to 35 minutes or until done.
- Cool the cake in the pan on a wire rack for 10 minutes. Remove from the pan.
- Drizzle the glaze on top of the warm cake.

GLAZE

- In a medium bowl, combine the confectioners' sugar, milk, and vanilla until smooth.

Serves 12 to 24

UPSIDE-DOWN PINEAPPLE CAKE

1/2 cup (1 stick) butter

1 cup brown sugar, packed

1 (20-ounce) can pineapple slices, drained

1 (6-ounce) can cherries, whole and drained

1 box cake mix—yellow, butter, or pineapple

- Preheat the oven to 350 degrees.
- Melt the butter in a 13 x 9 x 2-inch baking pan in the oven, removing when melted.
- Sprinkle the brown sugar evenly over the melted butter.
- Arrange the pineapple slices on top of the brown sugar.
- Place a cherry in the center of each pineapple slice.
- Using the ingredients listed on the cake box, prepare the cake mix. Blend as directed.
- Pour the prepared cake mix on top of the pineapple slices.
  Important: Do not stir.
- Bake at 350 degrees for 45 to 50 minutes or until done.
- Let the cake cool in the pan for about 10 minutes. Remove from the pan.
  Note: The pineapple slices should be on top.

Serves 12 to 24

Strong

WHEN YOUR WORLD SEEMS TO TURN UPSIDE-DOWN,

STAY STRONG. YOU CAN OVERCOME ANYTHING IN

LIFE WITH UNFALTERING INNER STRENGTH.

OTHER DESSERTS

APPLE CHARLOTTE

APPLES

4 large apples, cored and sliced

1/3 cup sugar

1 tablespoon cinnamon

3 tablespoons water

1 tablespoon butter

CRUMB TOPPING

1 cup flour

2 tablespoons butter, melted

1/2 cup light brown sugar, packed

APPLES

- Preheat the oven to 375 degrees.

- Place the sliced apples onto the bottom of a 13 x 9 x 2-inch baking pan coated with cooking spray.

- Sprinkle the sugar and cinnamon on top of the apples.

  Tip: If using tart apples, add 1/3 cup more sugar to sweeten.

- Pour the water over the apples, and dot with butter.

- Prepare the crumb topping, and sprinkle over the apples.

- Bake at 375 degrees for 50 to 55 minutes.

- Serve with your favorite vanilla ice cream, if desired.

CRUMB TOPPING

- In a small bowl, combine the flour, melted butter, and brown sugar. Stir well.

Serves approximately 12

Innocence

INNOCENCE IS PROFOUND.

純潔

Hope

WHEN FEELING BLUE AND TOSSED AROUND, GET SOME

REST AND HOPE FOR A BETTER TOMORROW. 希望

BLUEBERRY SALAD

GELATIN MIXTURE

2 (3 ounces each) packages
grape gelatin
2 cups boiling water
1 (20-ounce) can crushed
pineapple, undrained
1 (21-ounce) can blueberry
pie filling

TOPPING

1 (8-ounce) package cream cheese,
softened
1/2 cup sugar
1/2 cup sour cream
1/2 teaspoon vanilla
1/2 cup nuts, chopped

GELATIN MIXTURE

- In a 2-quart casserole dish or a large bowl, dissolve the gelatin with the boiling water.

- Add the pineapple and blueberry pie filling.

- Stir the mixture until thoroughly dissolved.

- Refrigerate for several hours until firm.

- When the gelatin mixture is firm, prepare the topping, and spread over the chilled gelatin.

- Cover and refrigerate until ready to serve. Refrigerate the leftovers.

TOPPING

- In a medium mixing bowl, beat the cream cheese, sugar, sour cream, and vanilla until well blended.

- Fold in the nuts.

Serves 16 to 20

CHOCOLATE-COVERED STRAWBERRIES

6 squares (12 ounces) chocolate-flavored bark coating
2 pints strawberries, whole with stems intact

- Rinse the strawberries, and dry thoroughly.

- In a large nonstick saucepan on the stovetop, melt the chocolate bark over low heat.

- Stir constantly, until smooth. Remove from heat.

- Immediately dip the strawberries, one at a time, into the melted chocolate.

  Variation: Dip the entire strawberry (except for the stem), or just one side.

- Place the dipped strawberries onto a baking sheet covered with wax paper.

- Place the baking sheet in the refrigerator until ready to serve.

- Refrigerate the leftovers.

Yields 2 pints

Job Well Done

YOU DESERVE A TOAST FOR A JOB WELL DONE—CHEERS TO YOU!

幹的好

FRUIT COBBLER

1/4 cup (1/2 stick) butter
1 cup sugar
1 cup flour
1 cup milk
2 teaspoons baking powder
2 to 3 cups fresh fruit—peaches (peeled and sliced),
   strawberries (stemmed and sliced), or blackberries (whole)

- Preheat the oven to 350 degrees.

- Melt the butter in a 13 x 9 x 2-inch baking pan in the oven,
  removing when melted.

- In a medium bowl, combine the sugar, flour, milk, and baking powder.

- Pour the batter on top of the butter. *Important: Do not stir.*

- Pour the fruit on top of the batter. *Important: Do not stir.*

- Bake at 350 degrees for 40 to 45 minutes or until golden brown.

- Serve warm with your favorite vanilla ice cream, if desired.

Serves 10 to 12

Blessings

SOMETIMES UNPLEASANT EXPERIENCES ARE BLESSINGS

IN DISGUISE. 祝福

PINK DESSERT

1 (8-ounce) container frozen whipped topping, slightly thawed

1 (14-ounce) can sweetened condensed milk

1 (20-ounce) can crushed pineapple, drained

1 (21-ounce) can pie filling (cherry or strawberry)

OPTIONAL

1/2 cup nuts, chopped

1 cup miniature marshmallows

- In a large mixing bowl, combine the whipped topping, sweetened condensed milk, pineapple, and pie filling.

- Stir well by hand.

- Add the optional ingredients, if desired.

- Cover and refrigerate until firm (at least 1 hour) before serving.

- Refrigerate the leftovers.

Serves approximately 12

正直

STAND OUT—

AND HAVE INTEGRITY

INSTEAD OF BLENDING

IN WITH THE CROWD.

THE RESULTS MAY

SURPRISE YOU.

Integrity

Knowledge

KNOWLEDGE NOT SHARED IS KNOWLEDGE WASTED.

RICE PUDDING

2 cups rice, cooked

1/4 **cup sugar**

2/3 **cup milk**

1 egg, slightly beaten

1/2 **teaspoon cinnamon**

1/4 **cup raisins**

2 tablespoons butter

1 teaspoon vanilla

111

- Preheat the oven to 375 degrees.

- In a large mixing bowl, combine the cooked rice, sugar, milk, egg, cinnamon, raisins, butter, and vanilla until well blended.

- Pour the rice mixture into a 9 x 5 x 3-inch loaf pan coated with cooking spray.

- Bake at 375 degrees for 30 minutes or until light brown.

Note: This also nicely complements a meal as a side dish.

Serves 4 to 6

SPICY PUMPKIN BREAD

1 1/2 cups sugar
1 1/2 cups brown sugar, packed
1 cup unsweetened applesauce
3 eggs
1 (16-ounce) can pumpkin
3 cups flour
1/2 teaspoon cloves
1 teaspoon cinnamon
1 teaspoon nutmeg
1 teaspoon baking soda
1/2 teaspoon salt
1/2 teaspoon baking powder
1 teaspoon vanilla
1 cup nuts, chopped

- Preheat the oven to 350 degrees.
- In a large mixing bowl, beat the sugar, brown sugar, and applesauce.
- Add the eggs and pumpkin.
- Combine the dry mixture—flour, cloves, cinnamon, nutmeg, baking soda, salt, and baking powder—in another large bowl.
- Gradually combine the dry mixture with the pumpkin mixture. Blend well.
- Add the vanilla, then fold in the nuts.
- Divide the batter equally between two prepared 9 x 5 x 3-inch loaf pans.
- Bake at 350 degrees for 65 to 70 minutes or until done.
- Cool each loaf in its pan on a wire rack for 10 minutes.
- Turn the loaves onto wire racks and cool completely.

Tip: To ease removal from the pan, use a dull knife to cut around the edges.

Yields 2 loaves

Meditation

STEP BACK FROM YOUR BUSY DAY TO GIVE TIME TO
YOURSELF IN THE FORM OF MEDITATION OR PRAYER.

WAFER BANANA PUDDING

1/2 **cup flour**
1/4 **teaspoon salt**
1/2 **teaspoon vanilla**
2 **tablespoons butter**
2/3 **cup sugar**
2 **cups milk**
2 **egg yolks, slightly beaten**
1 **to 2 cups vanilla wafers**
2 **bananas, sliced**
1/4 **cup nuts, chopped**

114

- In a large saucepan on the stovetop, combine the flour, salt, vanilla, butter, sugar, milk, and egg yolks until well blended.
  Tip: Use a wire whisk to remove the lumps before the pudding thickens.
- Cook over medium heat, stirring constantly, until the mixture thickens (about 7 minutes).
- Remove from heat.
- In a medium bowl, layer the wafers on the bottom.
  Tip: If you have any remaining wafers, use them for decoration.
- Layer the bananas over the wafers.
- Layer the pudding over the bananas.
- Sprinkle the nuts on top of the pudding.
- Cool the Wafer Banana Pudding, then refrigerate until ready to serve.
- Refrigerate the leftovers.

Serves 6 to 8

Mind

AN OPEN MIND HOLDS NO BOUNDARIES.

心靈

YOUR DESTINY DESSERT

Destiny

EACH OF US HAS A UNIQUE DESTINY. OUR TASK IS TO FIGURE OUT WHICH SPECIAL INGREDIENTS WE HAVE TO MAKE OUR OWN LIFE RECIPE.

HAVE FUN CREATING YOUR OWN DESTINY . . .

A Special Thanks

Alvin & Dorothy Blazek & Family

Ann Farkas

Blake Carter

Charles & Rose Boerner

David, Joan, Paul, Monica, Gregory, & Timothy Blazek

Deeva Lewis

Douglas Tsai

Frank & Cecilia

Frank Stanley Gove

Janet Blazek

Jay Love

Jennifer & Jason

Keith Crabtree

Michelle Dawn Elliott

Mindy Reed

Mun-Jo Jung

Phil, Stacie, & Luke

Rick, Rita, Aaron, & Shelby Gallaway

Scott, Brenda, & Ashlyn Blazek

The Carter Family

Vicki Gentile

Hints

GENERAL HINTS

For Proper Refrigeration
Certain desserts require refrigeration. Be sure to refrigerate any dessert with a milk- or egg-based filling, whipped topping, or cream cheese. When in doubt, refrigerate.

Baking Time May Vary
Since the baking time may vary from oven to oven, monitor the desserts frequently for readiness while baking.

To Soften Butter and Cream Cheese
To soften, remove the butter or cream cheese from the refrigerator at least 10 minutes before use. Be careful not to leave these ingredients at room temperature for too long.

To Slightly Beat Eggs
After cracking the eggs and removing their shells, place the eggs into a small bowl and beat slightly with a fork.

CANDY & COOKIE HINTS

To Test for Soft-Ball Stage When Making Candy
If you do not have a candy thermometer, you can still test for the soft-ball stage. Simply fill a cup with cold water, and place a drop of the hot candy mixture into the water. If the candy mixture forms a ball when dropped into the water, it is ready. If it does not, continue cooking the candy, retesting frequently.

To Store Candy
Use wax paper between the layers of candies to prevent sticking while storing. Store the candy in an airtight container in a cool place.

Humidity May Affect Certain Candies
Some candies turn out sticky on humid days, specifically Divinity and Sweet Kisses. If possible, avoid making these desserts on very humid days.

To Stop Cookies from Sticking to the Baking Sheet
When baking cookies, coat the baking sheet with cooking spray to prevent sticking.

To Bake Nicely Shaped Cookies
When dropping cookie dough onto a baking sheet, be sure to leave enough space (about an inch all around) between the cookies. This allows the cookies to expand when baking without colliding with one another.

To Cool Cookies
After removing the cookies from the oven, leave them on the pan for about a minute to set. Then remove to a wire rack to cool completely.

PIE HINTS

To Prepare Frozen Fruit for Use
If using frozen fruit, be sure to thaw and drain the fruit before using.

To Dot Fruit with Butter
Slice the butter into small pieces. Place the sliced butter on top of the fruit.

The Importance of Cutting Pie Slits
When placing a piecrust on top of a fruit filling, it is important to cut slits in this top piecrust. The slits allow steam to escape and prevent the piecrust from bubbling.

CAKE HINTS

For a Fluffy Cake
For a fluffy cake, separate the egg yolks and whites. Beat the egg yolks (if required) with the other ingredients. In a separate bowl, beat the egg whites until they are fluffy or until they form peaks. Fold the stiff egg whites into the batter.

To Prepare a Cake Pan
Grease the entire cake pan, including the bottom and sides, with shortening or butter. Sprinkle $1/4$ cup of flour over the shortening, ensuring that the entire pan is slightly coated with flour. Tap out the excess flour. Or simply coat a nonstick baking pan with cooking spray.

To Distribute Batter Equally
Before inserting a cake into the oven, slightly shake the batter-filled cake pan to distribute the batter evenly.

To Test a Cake for Readiness While Baking
Insert a cake tester (e.g., a wooden toothpick) into the center of the cake. If no batter sticks to the cake tester (or if it comes out "clean"), then the cake is ready.

To Remove a Cake from the Pan
Remove the cake from the oven, leaving it in the baking pan. Place the pan on a wire rack, and cool for approximately 10 minutes. Then place another wire rack upside down on top of the cake. Flip the cake, and remove the pan. Place the wire rack upside down again on the cake. Flip again. *Note: Some cakes do not need to be flipped twice.*

Index

121

122

O

P

R

123

About the Authors

The authors, Frances Blazek and Joyce Carter, are sisters and native Texans. They grew up on a farm along with their other seven siblings and beloved parents.

Frances received her Bachelor of Business Administration degree from the University of Texas at Arlington. She is a seasoned professional with diverse experience in the Information Technology sector. Frances enjoys baking, traveling, gardening, and working with youth.

Joyce earned her Bachelor of Arts degree at Harvard University and her Master of Business Administration at the McCombs School of Business (the University of Texas at Austin). Her professional experience includes working in the entrepreneurial, venture capital, and investment banking arenas. Joyce enjoys traveling with her husband, playing with her two Labrador Retrievers, and entertaining family and friends.

The authors both have their favorite desserts—Frances' signature desserts are the Bonbons and Ranger Cookies, while Joyce's are the Fruit Cobbler and Chocolate-Covered Strawberries.

Order Information

Thank you for your interest in DESSERTS with Character.

Please visit our Web site at **www.blazenspires.com** to order your own copy or additional copies for your family and friends.